Columbus, Ohio

A PHOTOGRAPHIC PORTRAIT

PHOTOGRAPHY BY
Randall Lee Schieber

Photography © Randall Lee Schieber. All rights
reserved.

First published in the United States of America
by:

Twin Lights Publishers, Inc.
8 Hale Street
Rockport, Massachusetts 01966
Telephone: (978) 546-7398
http://www.twinlightspub.com

ISBN: 1-885435-78-9
ISBN: 978-1-885435-78-1

10 9 8 7 6 5 4 3 2 1

Capitol Square (opposite)

The Ohio State Capitol's Greek Revival style
building is located in downtown Columbus.
The Vern Riffe Center for Government and the
Arts and the Hunting Center office complex
are to its north.

(jacket front)

Broad Street Bridge and Columbus Skyline

(jacket back)

North Bank Park

Images on pages 60–61 are courtesy of the
Motorcycle Hall of Fame.

Editorial researched and written by:
Francesca and Duncan Yates
www.freelancewriters.com

Book design by:
SYP Design & Production, Inc.
www.sypdesign.com

Printed in China

4

When the glaciers melted in Ohio twelve thousand years ago, their rivers ran through the state like liquid gold, rushing to the Ohio River, the greatest tributary of the Mississippi. They left in their wake the richest farmland and forests in America.

Columbus was founded in 1812 on Wolf's Ridge, a high bank of the Scioto River, an Ohio River tributary. Located in the geographic heart of the state, Columbus proved to be the perfect choice as a capital city.

When the first railroad came to Columbus in the 1850's, the city was energized as a Midwest transportation hub and soon became known internationally for distribution and manufacturing. Since then, Columbus has never looked back.

Today, Columbus is one of the fastest growing cities in the country, with a metro area population of 1.7 million and a reputation as one of America's most livable cities. Columbus, the state's largest metropolis, is home to 100,000 college students, half of which attend The Ohio State University, the largest state university system in the country. Headquarters for five major insurance companies, it also nurtures a growing industry of research and technology companies.

Columbus, or *The Discovery City*, is proud of its year-round festivals, professional and collegiate sports teams and acclaimed cultural venues. A revitalized downtown with gentrified historic, residential neighborhoods, a new Arena District, and the vibrant arts district, *Short North*, are just some of the many unique characteristics that draw so many to live, work and play in this great city.

Photographer Randall Lee Schieber, a long-time resident of Columbus, captures the very character of this vibrant city with spectacular images that tell the story of our country's heartland, where American values have built one of the country's most eminent cities.

Navstar Sculpture

A trio of enormous, gleaming sails of the Navstar sculpture in Franklin Park are filled with the winds of discovery in this graceful salute to Christopher Columbus. Its largest sail points to the North Star. The sculpture was created by acclaimed Ohio artist, Stephen Canneto.

Alexander Park *(opposite)*

Bicyclists enjoy a mild autumn day along the Scioto River Greenway as it meanders through Alexander Park. Located on the downtown riverfront, the park is dedicated to Arvin J. Alexander, city council president and visionary who was devoted to the betterment of the city.

Goodale Park Gazebo *(above)*

In 1851, Dr. Lincoln Goodale, Columbus' first doctor, donated this park to the people of the city. Used as a camp for Union troops during the Civil War, the park is surrounded by Victorian Village, a charming neighborhood featuring extraordinary examples of Victorian architecture.

Inniswood Metro Gardens

Part of the Metro Parks system of Columbus, the ethereal public gardens of Inniswood blossom in a pristine nature preserve that covers over one-hundred acres of woodlands, streams, and fields. Walking trails meander through wildflowers, roses, daffodils, hostas, and herbs.

A Seat in the Garden

Grace and Mary Innis donated their home
and land to the city in 1972. Since then,
Inniswood Metro Gardens has become
a place of tranquility and beauty for the
people of Columbus. The gardens include
healing herbs that have been used since
ancient times.

Franklin Park Conservatory

The Franklin Park Conservatory has been a Columbus jewel since 1895. The palatial Victorian conservatory introduced botanical gardens to Columbus. Several greenhouses display vegetation from diverse climates, such as the Himalayan Mountains, rainforests, and deserts.

10

Rainy Day in Schiller Park

Created by sculptor Joan Wobst, this whimsical fountain graces the gardens of Schiller Park. The park is the beautifully landscaped focal point of German Village, a neighborhood settled in the mid 1800's. The historic district has over 1,600 architecturally significant homes and businesses.

Torchiere *(opposite)*

Franklin Park Conservatory became one of the few institutions in the world to permanently house a major signature collection of Dale Chihuly's art when they purchased their 2003–2004 exhibit of the world renowned artist's work, including *Chandeliers* and *Torchiere*.

Niijima Floats *(above)*

Art and nature coexist at Franklin Park Conservatory with sculptor Dale Chihuly's work entitled, *Niijima*. The colorful glass orbs, inspired by Japanese fishing floats, bob in a pool of Asian koi, while glistening clusters of glass lilies majestically rise among real flowers.

The Art of Topiary

Artist James Mason's unique topiary landscape is a recreation of the 1886 masterpiece *A Sunday on the Isle of La Grande Jatte*
by French impressionist artist, Georges
Seurat. The garden sculptures include 54
figures, 8 boats, 3 dogs, a cat, and a mon-
key, all enhancing a tranquil pond.

Topiary Treasures

The vision of sculptor and Columbus native, James Mason, became a reality as he and his wife, Elaine, transformed the charred rubble of a former school for the deaf into one of Ohio's most beautiful attractions.

Field of Corn

The Sam and Eulalia Frantz Park in Dublin, Ohio, is dedicated to farmer, Sam Frantz, who once used the land to develop varieties of hybrid corn. Sculptor Malcolm Cochran commemorates Dublin's agricultural heritage with a field of over one-hundred concrete corn sculptures.

16

Leatherlips

Commissioned by the Dublin Arts Council, this limestone monument by Boston artist Ralph Helmick, honors the great Wyandot Native American leader, Sha-Te-Yah-Ron-Ya, who was referred to by local settlers as "Chief Leatherlips" because he was trusted to never break a promise.

Battelle Riverfront Park

A fanciful unicorn kneels gracefully in Battelle Riverfront Park. It is one of six bronze wildlife pieces in the park by artist, Jack Greaves. Battelle is a lovely green oasis with a panoramic view of the city and Scioto River.

Heritage Garden

A tour of the Governor's Residence includes a stroll through the award-winning Heritage Garden. Conceptualized by Hope Taft, wife of former Governor Bob Taft, the garden is divided into distinct areas, each with plants and flowers representing specific geographic locations across Ohio.

Butterfly in the Garden

The Franklin Park Conservatory's "Blooms
and Butterflies" exhibit includes over
100 varieties of local and exotic butterfly
species, among fragrant and tropical
blooms.

Columbus Park of Roses

One of the largest rose gardens in the country, the Columbus Park of Roses within Whetstone Park, has over ten thousand rose bushes. Since opening in 1953, there have been many improvements and additions to the park including herb and perennial beds.

The Rose in Bloom *(above)*

The highly-acclaimed Columbus Park of
Roses is 13 acres of fragrant beauty. It was
once the headquarters of the Amerian
Rose Society. *USA Today* honored the rose
garden with the top position in an interna-
tional listing of "Ten places to admire the
bloom on the rose."

Sweet Showers *(opposite)*

A pair of adventurous young girls cool off
under a sprinkler in the Columbus Park of
Roses. The site hosts an annual Rose
Festival attended by hundreds of garden
lovers. Weddings and other events are
held regularly at the garden's gazebo.

Hayden Run Falls *(above)*

Hayden Run creates a scenic gorge and waterfall in the middle of a Columbus suburb. Three unique plant species that flourish on the gorge walls are the rare Maidenhair Fern, Purple Cliffbrake Fern, and the Spreading Rock Cress, a state endangered plant species.

Camp Chase Confederate Cemetery *(opposite)*

The Camp Chase Confederate Cemetery is the final resting place of 2,260 Confederate soldiers who died here as prisoners of war. At the turn of the 20th century, public donations built the memorial arch over a large boulder, a landmark of the cemetery. Atop the arch is a bronze statue of a Confederate private, facing south. Legend has it that the cemetery is haunted by the "Lady in Gray," who still brings fresh flowers to the grave of Confederate soldier Benjamin Allen.

Santa Maria

The colorfully illuminated ship on the city's waterfront is hailed as the world's most authentic, museum-quality replica of Christopher Columbus' famous flagship, the *Santa Maria*. Along with its two companion ships, the *Nina* and the *Pinta*, the 98-foot sailing vessel made an historic crossing of the Atlantic Ocean in 1492 that would forever change the world. Guided tours onboard demonstrate the difficult living conditions aboard this surprisingly small wooden ship.

Columbus Arts Festival

Hundreds of white tents line the riverfront and the Town Street Bridge for the world-famous Columbus Arts Festival. The festival attracts more than 250,000 people over a three day period. Visitors come to view and purchase some of the region's best craft and visual artists' creative work.

The Arena District

The Arena District depicts layers of history as the old makes way for the new. The Union Station Arch stands as a constant reminder of Columbus' historic roots, while the new sports arena represents the city's ongoing modern evolution.

The Enduring Union Station Arch

The arch is the only remaining piece of Columbus' magnificent Union Station. Renowned Chicago architect, David Burnham, designed the train station in 1893 in the popular Beaux-Arts Classicism style. The regal arch now resides in McFerson Commons, a small park in the Arena District, several hundred feet from the site of the long-gone train station. It is a memorial to the golden days of the railroads and the stately architecture of the past.

Nationwide Arena

Hot Spot *(opposite, top and bottom)*

When Nationwide Arena was built, it became the centerpiece for the new Arena District, which has quickly become the city's hot, new downtown area. Trendy restaurants, popular night spots, live entertainment, apartment complexes, condominiums, office buildings, and parks create a vibrant neighborhood core. Outdoors, a giant video board lights up the district with music videos, short films, and district news.

Nationwide Arena *(above)*

Columbus' new Nationwide Arena is the showplace of the Arena District. Home to the National Hockey League's Blue Jackets, it also hosts concerts and shows. An open atrium, expansive lobbies, and concourses help fans stay in touch with the action.

31

North Bank Park (*opposite*)

Illuminated fountains dance in the cool
early evening at North Bank Park. This
scenic, downtown park on the Scioto
River is part of the Scioto Mile, a system
of bike trails, pedestrian paths, and green
ways that follow along the river to the
Whittier Peninsula.

Columbus Skyline (*above*)

The view from the Smith Brothers
Building reveals the main thoroughfares
and skyline of Columbus, the largest city
in Ohio with over 700,000 residents.
Located in the geographic center of the
state, it was founded in 1812 where the
Scioto and Olentangy rivers merge.

Red, White and Boom!

The most extravagant Fourth of July celebration in the Midwest is held on July 3rd in Columbus, so as not to compete with planned festivities of nearby communities and towns on the 4th. The all-day event includes a parade, live music, plenty of food, and a spectacular fireworks display.

Columbus Celebrates

The dramatic lines of the LeVeque Tower are silhouetted against a spectacular fireworks display during Columbus' famous Fourth of July festivities. Dressed for the holiday with red, white, and blue lights, this landmark 1927 art deco building was the city's tallest building until 1973.

Hyatt Regency Hotel *(above)*

Resting atop massive columns, the clean, de-constructionist lines of the Hyatt Regency Hotel create a dramatic setting in downtown Columbus. The hotel is connected to the Greater Columbus Convention Center.

Vern Riffe Center *(opposite)*

One of the newest skyscrapers in the city skyline, the Vern Riffe Center for Government and the Arts is a state office building and a performing arts complex. On the ground level, it houses the internationally acclaimed Riffe Center Theatre Complex with four, state-of-the-art theaters, includ-ing the Capitol Theatre, a premier performance venue that regularly features comedy, family entertainment, music, dance, theater, and cultural programming. Many of the city's performing arts groups play here.

Skyline from Genoa Park

A statue of Columbus' founding father,
Lucas Sullivant, stands proudly in Genoa
Park overlooking the modern city that was
founded over 200 years ago. The statue
was erected in 2000, as part of the
Columbus Bicentennial celebration.

Founding Father of Columbus

Lucas Sullivant, a young surveyor from Virginia, founded a permanent settlement on the west bank of the Scioto River in 1797 and called it Franklinton. As time passed the growing city of Columbus encompassed the site.

Water Play *(top and bottom)*

One of the favorite features of North Bank
Park is the unique, interactive fountain on
the upper plaza. Located along the Scioto
River, it is a busy place on a hot, summer
day where children frolic in the fountain
and the fountain plays right back.

North Bank Park

North Bank Park, in downtown Columbus, features beautifully landscaped trails for walking and cycling. The park is part of the Scioto Mile, an area comprised of trails, parks and revitalized neighborhoods in the downtown area.

Greater Columbus Convention Center *(top)*

A world-class convention and meeting facility, the downtown location of the Greater Columbus Convention Center makes it convenient to unlimited cultural, entertainment, dining, and shopping experiences, including the center's own food court and shops.

Franklin County Veterans Memorial *(bottom)*

The recently expanded Veterans Memorial has over 100,000 square feet of exhibit space and meeting rooms. Its spacious 4,000-seat auditorium has welcomed legendary performers such as Elvis, Bob Dylan, and Bruce Springsteen.

Capitol Square Explorer *(opposite)*

Against the backdrop of the Vern Riffe Center for Government and the Arts, stands a statue of the city's namesake, Christopher Columbus, located in Capitol Square.

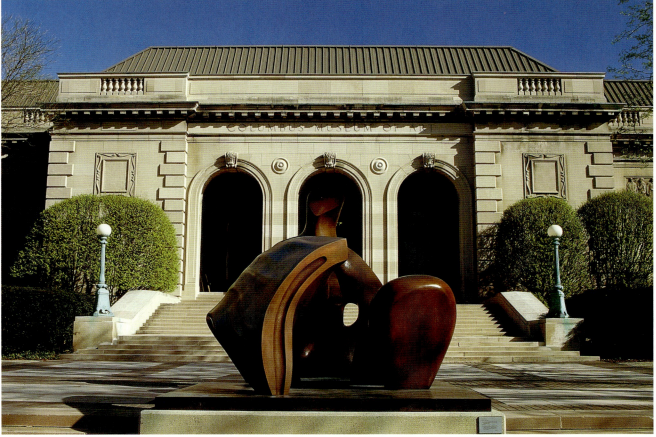

Discovery District *(opposite, top)*

Discovery District is the name given to the downtown area of Columbus that encompasses the greatest concentration of arts and educational institutions in the city, including the Columbus Museum of Art, the Columbus College of Art and Design, and the amazing Topiary Park.

Columbus Museum of Art *(opposite, bottom)*

Founded in 1878, the Columbus Museum of Art is recognized internationally for its impressive collection of late 19th- and early 20th-century American and European modern art, as well as its outstanding collection of works by regional artists.

Russell Page Sculpture Garden *(above)*

Covering an entire city block, the magnificent sculpture garden of the Columbus Museum of Art features major works by Calder, Moore, Marcks, Hepworth, Maillol, Manzu, Meadmore, Rickey and others. The garden was designed by noted landscape architect Russell Page.

45

One Columbus Center

The staggered design of this distinctive office building creates fifteen corner offices for every floor. Built in 1987, the twenty-six-floor building features a walkway on the second level of the garage that connects to the famous art deco skyscraper, LeVeque Tower.

Wexner Center for the Arts *(above and left)*

The Ohio State University's Wexner Center is a research laboratory for the arts with cutting-edge exhibitions, films, and performances. The architecturally acclaimed facility provides a nurturing environment for the creative spirit.

Galleries on High Street *(opposite)*

Art galleries line the blocks along High Street, the center of Columbus' art district. In the distance, a giant soccer ball sculpture hovers on a building's side, a graphic celebration of the Columbus Crew, the city's professional soccer team.

City Hall

After Columbus' original City Hall was destroyed by fire in 1921, this stately Neoclassical building was designed as the first part of the city's new civic center. Errected in 1928, the City Hall occupies an entire block.

Christopher Columbus

In 1955, when Columbus, Ohio became a sister-city to Genoa, Italy, the birthplace of the famous explorer, the people of Genoa bestowed upon the city, a statue of Christopher Columbus. The sculpture stands proudly in front of City Hall.

Senate Building (above)

The dazzling, new Senate Building and Atrium were finished in 1993 and spurred extensive renovations and restorations in the antiquated Statehouse. All Capitol Square tours begin at the Atrium's Visitors Center.

State House Rotunda (left)

The magnificent Rotunda rises 120 feet from the ground to the stained glass sky-light with a hand-painted Seal of Ohio in its center. The spectacular floor is designed with nearly 5,000 pieces of hand-cut marble from around the world.

Grand Stair Hall (opposite)

The extensive restoration of the State-house to its former glory was cause for celebration. Twenty-thousand citizens attended the grand re-opening as Civil War cannons fired and military jets flew overhead.

The Ohio Theatre (above)

Owned and operated by the Columbus Association for the Performing Arts (CAPA), this historic landmark was saved from the wrecking ball and restored after citizens raised over $2 million dollars. Today, it is the elegant home of the Columbus Symphony Orchestra, BalletMet, and The Broadway Series. In addition to the Ohio Theatre, CAPA owns and operates the Palace Theatre and The Southern Theatre.

Palace Theatre (left)

Designed in the style of France's Palais de Versailles, the Palace Theatre is an architectural treasure with its majestic lobby. Its busy schedule includes concerts, special events and the "Broadway in Columbus" series.

The Southern Theatre (opposite)

Opened in 1896, The Southern's stage has been graced by the Barrymores, Bernhardt, and Jolson. Restored in 1998, the nearly perfect acoustics make it the treasured home of the Columbus Jazz Orchestra, Chamber Music Columbus, and Pro-Musica Chamber Orchestra. The theater is connected to the Westin Great Southern Hotel.

Discovering Heritage

Built in 1926, the landmark Pythian Temple was re-dedicated in 1987 in honor of Dr. Martin Luther King, Jr. It is the only historic structure in the city that was designed by an African-American architect, Samuel Plato.

Martin Luther King Performing and Cultural Arts Complex

The mission of The King Arts Complex is "to preserve and celebrate the cultural and artistic heritage of African-Americans and the African-American experience, while developing greater understanding and harmony among all people."

Center of Science and Industry *(above)*

COSI celebrates curiosity with interactive exhibits to help chidren have fun while learning about the world around them. There is a special *Kidspace*, just for infants, toddlers, and pre-schoolers. Since 1964, nineteen-million visitors have come to the center to explore and play.

Underwater Discoveries *(opposite)*

Scepter in hand, Poseidon, God of the Sea, rises out of an ocean of lights in this fantastic, interactive oceanic exhibit at the Center of Science and Industry. Children can generate waves in a wave tank and shoot off water cannons while disovering the mysteries of the deep.

Motocross America

The exciting history of Motocross is traced in "Motocross America," an exhibit featuring great bikes from the last five decades. Choice ephemera, photos, cutaway engines, historical racing apparel, and rare pedigree motorcycles bring the story to life.

SuperMann

Dick Mann was more than a great American motorcycle racer. He also tuned his own bikes, helped several manufacturers with their chassis designs and later in life organized vintage motorcycle racing. In "SuperMann", the interesting story is told and supported with over a dozen unique and pedigree bikes including two Daytona 200 winners.

Ohio Historical Center *(opposite, top)*

The Ohio Historical Society oversees sixty historic sites and museums throughout the state. Its premiere museum, the Ohio Historical Center, regularly updates exhibits and provides rich resources for local genealogists and archeologists.

Jack Nicklaus Museum *(opposite, bottom)*

Jack Nicklaus' hometown is the site of a museum dedicated to the golfing great. Located at The Ohio State University's sports complex, the 23,000-square-foot facility takes golfing enthusiasts through the history of the sport as well as Nicklaus' unparalleled accomplishments.

Art on the Skyline *(above)*

This 100-foot-tall sculpture enhances the campus of the Columbus College of Art and Design, located in the Discovery District. It was designed by Artglo Company employee, Doris Shlayn, and donated by Artglo. The linear typographic work has become a city landmark.

Easton Town Center

The most modern neighborhood in Columbus, Easton, is home to the Easton Town Center shopping complex that features retail, dining, and entertainment venues. The center's ambiance is that of a small town, including green spaces with features that the whole family can enjoy.

Victorian Village

Now one of Columbus' trendier, downtown neighborhoods, the historic and charming Victorian Village has over one-thousand 19th-century houses and structures that are excellent examples of period architecture. Most have been lovingly restored and are meticulously maintained.

Novel Characters *(top)*

The home of James Thurber is a treasure trove of the famous author's most intimate possessions. In addition to original drawings, manuscripts, and first editions of his books, the grounds are delightfully dotted with characters from his stories.

Children's Stories *(bottom)*

The prolifically talented James Thurber was most recognized for *The Secret Life of Walter Mitty*, which depicted the stormy relationship of a meek, daydreaming husband and his shrewish wife, while their pets quietly observed their noisy altercations.

The Thurber House *(opposite)*

Widely considered to be the greatest humorist since Mark Twain, James Thurber, a Columbus native, lived here in this modest home with his parents during college. The house has been restored to represent the early part of the 20th century.

THE
THURBER
HOUSE

77

Victorian Lifestyle

The Kelton House Museum is a vintage Victorian home that showcases the 19th-century every-day life of the Keltons, who were abolitionists during the Civil War. The home was instrumental in the Underground Railroad, and at the family's request, is used for educational purposes.

The Kelton House Museum

The Kelton family home was part of the Underground Railroad, a network of human conveyance provided by those sympathetic to the abolition of slavery during the Civil War. The Keltons befriended two runaway slaves, Martha and Pearl. Martha stayed with the Kelton family, marrying Thomas Lawrence. For forty years, Thomas worked for the Keltons and the two families became very close friends.

Old Governor's Mansion

Built as a private home in 1904, architect
Frank Packard designed the estate in the
Georgian Revival Eclectic style. It was
purchased by the state of Ohio in 1917,
and served as the official governor's residence until 1957.

Style and Substance

This historic landmark was home to ten of Ohio's governors between 1917 and 1957, and served as the site of the Ohio Archives until 1970. It was later purchased from the state and housed a restaurant. Today it is the headquarters for The Columbus Foundation, a philanthropic organization.

Tribute to Ohio's Heros

The Ohio Veterans Plaza was originally inspired by an illegal, makeshift plywood memorial to Vietnam Veterans. Its purpose of honoring these brave heros was soon embraced by the state legislature resulting in a tribute to all armed forces from World War II veterans, to those who are yet to serve in the future. The curved limestone wall is inscribed with letters of servicemen to their loved ones.

Ohio Veterans Plaza *(above and pages 74–75)*

Dedicated in 1998 upon the completed renovations to Capitol Square, the Ohio Verterans Plaza serves as the east entrance to the statehouse grounds. In addition to the commemorative wall, the plaza contains plaques representing each of the armed services, as well as plaques and flags identifying each of Ohio's 88 counties, surrounding a lawn reminiscent of military parade grounds.

North Market *(above and opposite)*

Located in Short North since 1876, North Market is the last remaining enclosed public market in Central Ohio. It is home to local greengrocers, farmers, butchers, fishmongers, and bakers. Today, wares include gourmet groceries, gifts, and unique shops.

New Albany Classic Invitational Grand Prix *(above)*

The New Albany Classic is a non-profit fundraising event that draws top professional equestrians. Show events are held in New Albany, Ohio on the thousand-acre estate of Columbus businessman and philanthropist, Leslie "Les" H. Wexner.

Quarter Horse Congress *(opposite, top and bottom)*

The Quarter Horse Congress, the world's largest single-breed horse show, attracts over 650,000 people to the Ohio State Fairgrounds annually. This is the largest event in Ohio and the third largest convention in the country.

Bicentennial Park *(above)*

Bicentennial Park draws downtown residents and suburbanites to live performances, manicured gardens, and picnic areas with easy access to the Scioto River and Greenway Trail.

LeVeque Tower *(opposite)*

LeVeque Tower, a magnificent art deco skyscraper, was the first to be erected in Columbus. In its heyday, from 1927 until 1973, the 47-story masterpiece was the shining star of the skyline and the tallest building between New York and Chicago.

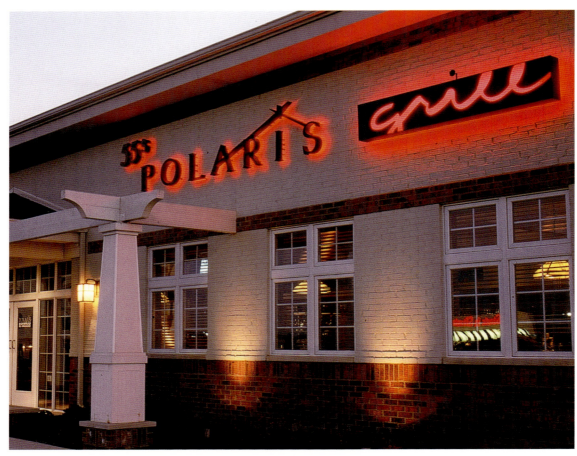

Polaris Grill (*opposite, top*)

Come early to avoid the crowds at Polaris' famous Sunday buffet. Formally a 55 Restaurant, patrons now come from all over Ohio to enjoy their signature "55" salad and to purchase a bottle of their private label salad dressing.

Polaris Fashion Place (*opposite, bottom*)

Central Ohio's largest mall, Polaris Fashion Place is comprised of 150 stores. The mall's lavish interior includes multiple common areas that are flooded with natural light.

Short North (*above*)

Goodale Street, located in the historic Short North district, is a hip locality that draws crowds from the Victorian and Italian Village, the business district, the Battille Institute, and students from Ohio State.

Short North Murals *(top and bottom)*

The art district of Columbus, known as, Short North and home to numerous galleries, is also famed for its many wall mural replicas of famous works. Artists Steve Galgas and Mike Altman created these two irreverent, but celebrated works.

Union Station Café (top)

Jeff and Greg Ackers created this ambitious mural on a 100-foot-long wall at Union Station Café. The talented artists also created a mural of the original Union Station on the wall of Utrect's, an art supply store.

The World is a Canvas (bottom)

In the Bohemian atmosphere of Short North, Columbus' art district, expect the unexpected on every street. Art is everywhere—inside galleries and shops, on street corners, and stretched across the massive walls of buildings.

Short North Galleries *(top and bottom)*

On the first Saturday of every month, Short North is open late for their "Gallery Hop." Galleries open new exhibitions and offer paté and port as street musicians play on. The streetscape is sophisticated yet fun; galleries rub shoulders with restaurants and stylish boutiques mingle with businesses.

The Art District *(opposite)*

Short North has become a world-class art district through an urban renaissance. For the city of Columbus, Short North is a sanctuary—a place of character where people can be charged and challenged, and where they can recycle energy back into the city through pure creativity.

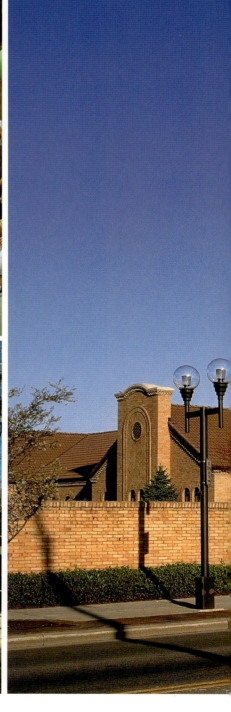

Greek Festival (*top*)

Columbus' Greek Festival, held every Labor Day weekend, is a celebration of the rich Greek heritage in the city. The event is highlighted with delicious ethnic foods, traditional dance, lively music, and exhibits centered on Greek tradition and culture.

Schmidt's (*bottom*)

Schmidt's Restaurant and Banquet Haus is an old German family business that began in 1886 in a brick livery stable during the period when German immigrants were settling in Columbus. This historic German Village eatery has a delicious menu of German and American foods and beers.

The Annunciation Greek Orthodox Cathedral

The distinctive lines of the Greek Orthodox Cathedral exemplify the traditional Byzantine style of architecture, which dates back to the sixth century AD. This impressive structure, located in the Short North district, is fashioned in the shape of a Greek cross with a dome rising from the juncture. Typical of that era, the cathedral's lavish interior has magnificent mosaics comprised of five-million tiles of Venetian glass, marble and 24-cart gold, sandwiched between two pieces of glass.

Traditions at German Village *(top, bottom and opposite)*

German Village is a unique place where immigrants came to establish new lives in the growing heartland of mid-nineteenth-century America. Period architecture is infused into the entire community. Residents value cultural traditions, passing them along from generation to generation.

A Festive Welcome

Houses and businesses in German Village celebrate the Christmas holidays with glorious lights, garlands and wreaths, indoors and out. Many holiday traditions originated from Germany, including the evergreen Christmas tree, tree lights, carols, and sweets.

Aisle of White Lights

German Village becomes a snow globe of Christmas spectacle around every corner, and along every cobblestone path. Night-time shopping, specialty drinks, food, carolers, juggling elves, and ten-thousand 'luminaria' light the path to a festive holiday season.

Worthington Village

Columbus' historic Worthington neighborhood exemplifies a true Dickensian Christmas. There are garlands, velvet bows, carolers, and shopkeepers who greet holiday customers and window shoppers alike, along High Street.

Christmas Tree Lighting

Worthington holds a traditional tree lighting ceremony on the Village Green after Thanksgiving. People from all over the metropolitan area come to witness the lighting that officially marks the start of the Christmas season.

Christmas at the Columbus Zoo

During the Christmas holidays, there are carolers and crackling campfires in huge barrels lighting up the night. Winter nights are for bundling up in Ohio although, the atmosphere at the zoo is cozy and inviting. Besides ice-skating and indoor exhibits like the aquarium and the Roadhouse, there are warm pretzels, wassail, thermal mugs of steamy hot chocolate, and roasted nuts.

A Luminous Holiday Palette

The Columbus Zoo becomes an electric palette of Christmas spectacle every year from mid-November through the New Year. Each night, the zoo keeps its doors open and illuminates the night with a spectacular display of thousands of Christmas lights, strung from one end of the zoo to the other. It's a real treat for children to talk with Santa Claus, surrounded by real reindeer, exotic creatures, and Christmas spirit all around.

Studies in Blue and Gray *(above and opposite)*

Shades of blue and gray are evident in these serene images from inside the Columbus Zoo. From 1978 to 1993, Director, Jack Hanna, oversaw the transformation of the zoo's environment away from caged enclosures to novel open spaces that reflected more natural habitats.

The Ohio State University *(above)*

U.S. News & World Report's rankings of undergraduate colleges in America currently places Ohio State as the best public university in Ohio, and one of the most successful in America.

William Oxley Thompson *(opposite)*

An ordained minister for half of his life, Dr. William Oxley Thompson later held the title of President of The Ohio State University from 1899–1925. The Thompson Library and the 11-foot statue of its namesake, pay tribute to the devoted Buckeye.

The Ohio State Campus

Founded in 1870, The Ohio State University is one of the largest universities in America with a student population of 50,000, and a faculty that includes Nobel laureates. *U.S. News & World Report* deemed it one of the top universities in the country.

Schottenstein Center

Located at The Ohio State University's Columbus campus, the Schottenstein Center is the home of the Buckeye basketball and men's hockey teams. The multipurpose arena hosts everything from sporting events to concerts and touring companies.

Big School, Big Game

The Ohio State Buckeyes have played their
home games in Ohio Stadium since 1922.
The winning football team is a member of
the Big Ten Conference. The Ohio State
University Marching Band is renowned for
their intricate formation of the word
"Ohio" in script during each game.

South Campus Gateway

Opened in 2005, this ambitious development project is adjacent to The Ohio State University campus. The Gateway serves the large student population with housing rentals, shopping, and entertainment, as well as professional office space.

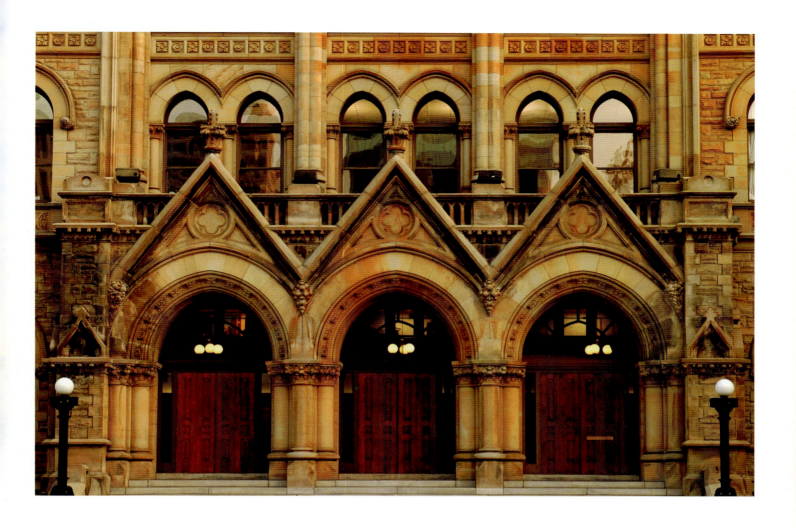

Orton Hall *(opposite)*

Opened in 1893, Orton Hall is one of the oldest remaining buildings on The Ohio State University campus. It is constructed of forty different types of native stone, laid in the order of their natural positions in Ohio's bedrock. So unique, it is a national historic landmark.

Old, Old Post Office *(above)*

Known as the "old, old post office," this spectacular, stately building adjacent to Capitol Square was Columbus' first federal building when completed in 1887. One of the few remaining 19th-century structures, the deteriorating building was saved by the efforts of the city's prestigious law firm, Bricker and Eckler, and lovingly restored to its former grandeur. Inside, the law firm's staff of 250 lawyers work amidst the historic beauty of a bygone era.

Golfing at Muirfield Village *(opposite, top)*

Jack Nicklaus designed and continues to manage this challenging course in the Columbus suburb of Dublin. Rated number seventeen in North America, the course has hosted the PGA Tour's Memorial Tournament since 1976.

Columbus Clippers *(opposite, bottom)*

In 1977, Franklin County Commissioner, Harold Cooper, resolved to bring a new baseball team and stadium to Columbus. The Clippers were the first minor league team to have a stadium with Astroturf. In 1998, the turf was replaced with real grass and a new scoreboard was installed.

Scioto Downs *(above)*

Racing fans fill the grandstand at Scioto Downs to watch harness racing's superstars jockey for first place. Harness racing has been a Columbus tradition for over 45 years.

The Cycling Classic *(top and bottom)*

Wendy's Restaurants sponsors the highly-
acclaimed Cycling Classic, a six-race
series that awards points to the top thirty
riders in each race. Headquarters for the
fast-food chain are located in Columbus.

The Columbus Marathon

Participants of the Columbus Marathon compete on a flat, fast course that encircles the city. The marathon and half-marathon attract nearly 8,000 runners. The race also features the Columbus Marathon Expo, a two-day attraction with over 70 sports and fitness booths.

Summer Refreshment *(above)*

The water park at Wyandot Lake has a wave pool, lazy-river tube ride, and body slides. The park recently merged with the Columbus Zoo and Aquarium and will undergo a $20-million-dollar renovation.

Hot Air Balloon Festival *(opposite, top)*

In September, the late-afternoon skies of Delaware County become dotted with hundreds of colorful hot air balloons. It is a grand spectacle of color and grace as the huge orbs ascend into the open and glide along the wide Ohio skies.

Columbus Arts Festival *(opposite, bottom)*

Columbus officially welcomes in the summer season with this much-anticipated event. The Columbus Arts Festival is held over four days, and is one of the nation's premier arts festivals with a wide variety of art exhibits and continuous live entertainment.

Alum Creek State Park *(top)*

Minutes from downtown Columbus, Alum
Creek State Park, set amidst the rolling
fields and woodlands surrounding the
reservoir, offers a wonderful variety of
outdoor activities for the millions who
visit every year.

Weekend Retreat *(bottom)*

Boats rest in the setting sun after a full day
on the water. Alum Creek features one of
the largest inland beaches in Ohio. Its
3,000-foot shoreline provides boating
docks, a concession stand, changing
facilities and scenic areas for picnicking
and grilling.

Afternoon Sail

From sailboats to runabouts, Alum Creek Lake is a popular Ohio boating venue and is home to the Alum Creek Sailing Association. The lake is also an excellent fishing spot, hosting a number of bass fishing tournaments.

Alum Creek Reservoir

Fishing enthusiasts prefer the quiet,
secluded coves of the northern shore, far
from the bustling water sports. In these
out-of-the-way corners, lines are cast in
hopes of catching record-breaking bass,
bluegill, crappie, walleye, and saugeye.

The Other Hoover Dam

This particular Hoover Dam is in Westerville, Ohio and is a major water source for Columbus. It dams the Big Walnut Creek and forms the Hoover Memorial Reservoir, a favorite spot for water sports and great fishing.

Fishing on Scioto River

The Scioto River, running through central and southern Ohio for over two-hundred miles, is well-known for great fishing. Anglers have a number of spots where they can catch white crappie, rock bass, bluegill, largemouth bass, catfish, saugeye and, of course, Ohio's official state fish, the smallmouth bass. The Scioto flows through Columbus where it is joined by the Olentangy River, its largest tributary. Further south, it meets the Ohio River.

Scioto River Sunset *(top and bottom)*

The sun drops low in the Columbus sky, reflecting lavender and salmon shades on the surface of the Scioto River. Life is sweet; the line tugs one last time and the feeling is pure contentment. Time to reel in, pack up the gear, salute the sunset, and head for home.

The Ohio State Fair *(opposite and above)*

An Ohio tradition for over 150 years, The Ohio State Fair is one of the largest state fairs in the country, attracting over 800,000 people annually to the Ohio Exposition Center on 17th Street. When the fair first began back in 1853, the only ride available was on the back of a slow pony. Today, the rides at the state fair are faster than ever, with giant roller coasters and rides that roll, spin, and drop, providing the very best in amusement park fun. Over twelve days of continuous excitement, the state of Ohio shows off its very best in agriculture, crafts, and fun.

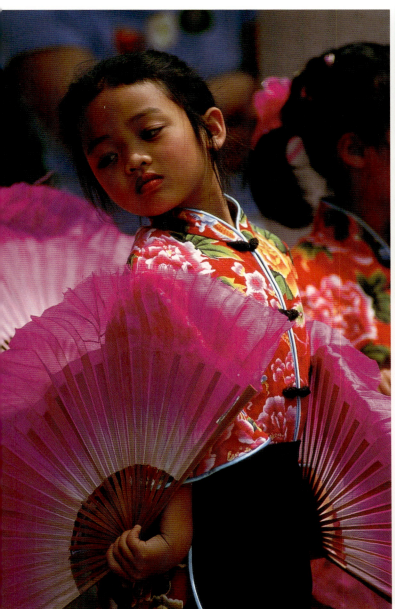

Oktoberfest (*opposite*)

Ken Nicol and Mary Drake perform at Oktoberfest, one of the top one-hundred events held in North America. Held at the tip of German Village proper, the traditional Oktoberfest is a plethora of native foods, shops, and music, with over sixty bands performing.

Asian Festival (*left and right*)

Beautiful traditional costumes and graceful, ancient dances are part of the authentic Asian cultural activities at this popular annual festival that attracts performers from all over the world. Asian foods and crafts round out the weekend event.

The Brewery District *(top)*

Founded by German immigrants during the early 1800s, the Brewery District, adjacent to German Village, began as a band of family-run breweries that prospered for decades. Today, the district is a thriving business and entertainment center, spanning 27 acres of vintage buildings.

ComFest Community Festival *(bottom)*

ComFest is a unique and proud thirty-five-year-old Columbus tradition. While a free music and arts festival, the event is also a major venue for organizations promoting peace and social justice in Ohio. The festival is run entirely by volunteers and has no corporate sponsors. The ultimate, competitive showcase for local musicians and artists, the festival features over two-hundred acts. Pictured above, from left to right, are Dave Workman, John Boerstler, and Johnny Ace.

The Jazz & Rib Festival

Live jazz al fresco heats up the stages at Bicentennial Park and the Riverfront Amphitheater with hot groups like Spyro Gyra, Liquid Soul, Dianne Reeves, and Lafayette Gilchrist. For twenty-seven years, record-breaking crowds have flocked to this outstanding musical extrav-aganza to hear some of the country's best jazz groups and savor mouth-watering ribs prepared by barbecue royalty.

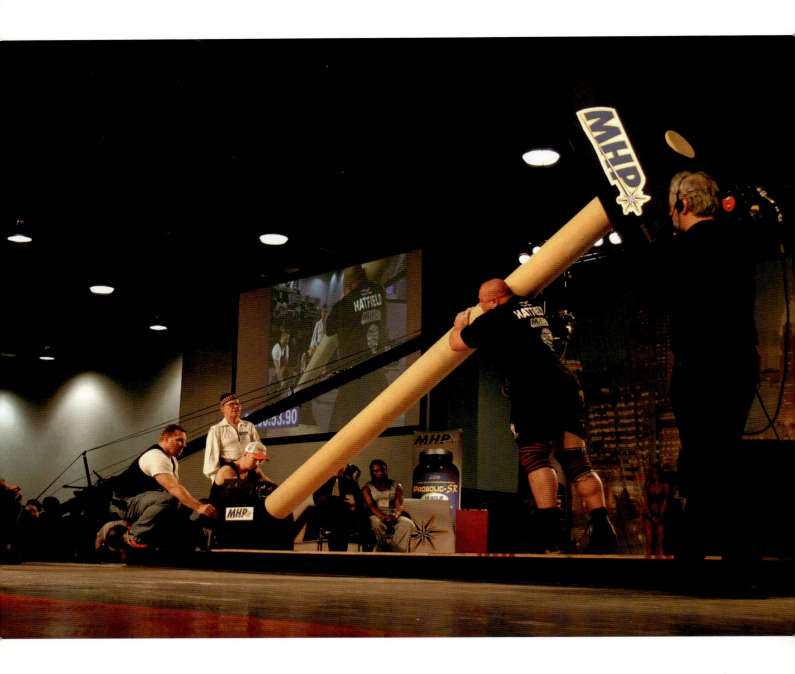

The Arnold Schwarzenegger Classic *(above)*

Every year the streets of Columbus are filled with thousands of top athletes, priming themselves for the world's largest and most prestigious body building and fitness competition as well as a variety of other sports including speed skating, gymnastics, and archery, to name a few.

Festival Latino *(opposite, top)*

Columbus hosts the largest Hispanic/Latino event in Ohio where authentic arts, crafts, foods, and live music make for a stimulating day. Revelers dance the night away in Bicentennial Park, enjoying a true Latino experience.

Doo Dah Parade *(opposite, bottom)*

Run completely by volunteers, the Fourth of July Doo Dah Parade attracts some of Columbus' funniest and most creative people who poke good-natured fun at everything and everyone.

127

Randall Lee Schieber

Randall Lee Schieber is a commercial photographer based in Columbus, Ohio specializing in editorial, location, landscape, and architectural photography. He has been shooting professionally for more than fifteen years.

Schieber was born in Findlay, Ohio and spent his early childhood in Mexico City. Since then, he has traveled widely throughout the United States and Mexico. He studied photography and art, first in Tucson, Arizona and later at The Ohio State University. He went on to earn a B. A. degree from Kent State University, Kent, Ohio.

Many of Schieber's images are on display at Columbus' Sears Distribution Center and McDonald's theme restaurants, as well as several Cleveland medical facilities. He has published numerous calendars on Columbus and is featured exclusively each year in the Ohio Scenic Calendar. Schieber currently has three books out on Ohio that showcase his work, *Ohio Simply Beautiful*, *Ohio Impressions*, and *Ohio Then and Now*. His work has appeared in many national and local publications, magazines, and newspapers including *Ohio Magazine*, *Midwest Living* and *The New York Times*. He has worked for a diverse list of corporations and organizations, some of which include McDonald's, Experience Columbus, Ohio Division of Travel and Tourism, The Audubon Society, The Great Lakes Publishing Company, Lucent Technologies, and Ruscilli Construction Co. Inc. To view more of Randall's work, please visit his web site at www.randallschieber.com.